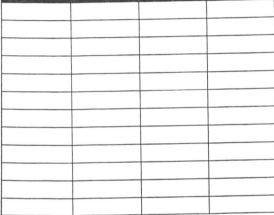

For Patrick,
my nephew-in-the-know, who led me to this story.

Special thanks to Iggy, Ben, and Eddie for sharing
their I-secrets. And high fives to Paula Manzanero,
the editor with the all-seeing-eye; Gabriel Cooper,
for his illuminating design; and copy editor Brandy
Colbert for keeping the book real.

PENGUIN WORKSHOP
Penguin Young Readers Group
An Imprint of Penguin Random House LLC

Photo credits: **Archives départementales d'Ille-et-Vilaine:** 61 (top). **Library of Congress:** 8, 18 (top), 19
(top, bottom), 30, 40, 41, 50, 59, 60 (top), 60–61, 80. **Los Angeles Times:** 83. **Missouri History Museum:** 33.
**NASA/Bill Ingalls:** 93 (bottom). **NASA/Goddard Space Flight Center Scientific Visualization Studio:**
92. **National Institute of Mental Health:** 9. **National Library of the Netherlands:** 26. **US Congress:** 69
(right). **US Department of Defense:** 69 (left). **Thinkstock:** cover, throughout interior (all-seeing eye vector
illustration): neyro2008/iStock, (triangle pattern): cienpies/iStock; 4, 5, 99 (hands): Sylversarts/iStock; 15
(bee): cosveta/iStock; 34 (compass): Olly molly/iStock; 36–37 (shepherd's crook): Cannasue/iStock; 38–39
(Confucius statue): Toncherd/iStock, (Plato statue): thegreekphotoholic/iStock; 43 (George Washington
head): ra3rn/iStock; 47 (lightbulb): DenPotisev/iStock; 62 (dollar bill): paulprescott72/iStock; 63 (seal):
DaddyBit/iStock; 71 (atomic bomb): Paul Campbell/iStock; 73 (Earth): Stockbyte; 81 (reptilian portrait):
LindaMarieB/iStock; 107 (flying saucer): oorka/iStock. **Wikimedia Commons:** 14; 18 (bottom); 21; 23;
24–25 (top): John Cornellier, (bottom): Brian Robert Marshall; 28–29 (Knights Templar, plan of Jerusalem,
twelfth century): National Library of the Netherlands; 32; 35; 48 (left): Daveleicuk, (right): Mark Howard
Brierley; 51; 57; 58; 67 (top): BoolaBoola2; 88 (Hollywood sign): Thomas Wolf, www.foto-tw.de / CC BY-SA
3.0; 93 (top): AgnosticPreachersKid.

Text copyright © 2018 by Sheila Keenan.
All rights reserved. Published by Penguin Workshop, an imprint of
Penguin Random House LLC, 345 Hudson Street, New York, New York 10014.
PENGUIN and PENGUIN WORKSHOP are trademarks of Penguin Books Ltd, and
the W colophon is a trademark of Penguin Random House LLC.
Manufactured in China.

Library of Congress Control Number: 2018016071

ISBN 9781524787936          10 9 8 7 6 5 4 3 2 1

# RAISE YOUR HAND IF YOU:

**HEARD THE ILLUMINATI IS SENDING SECRET MESSAGES THROUGH *ASSASSIN'S CREED***

▲

**THINK THE *I* IN APPLE GEAR *DOESN'T* STAND FOR *INTERNET***

▲

**SUSPECT SCOOBY-DOO, LORDE, ANDERSON COOPER, AND REPTILES HAVE SOMETHING IN COMMON**

# GIVE ME A SIGN IF YOU'VE EVER:

**DRAWN TWO TRIANGLES INSIDE EACH OTHER**

**HUMMED THE THEME SONG FROM *THE X-FILES***

**WHISPERED, "ILLUMINATI CONFIRMED"**

YEAH, YOU'RE READY FOR THE TRUTH. TURN THE PAGE . . .

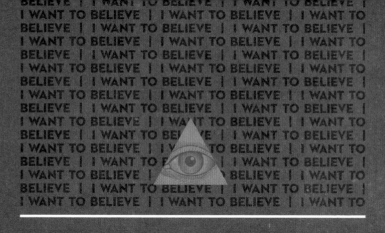

# I WANT TO
# BELIEVE

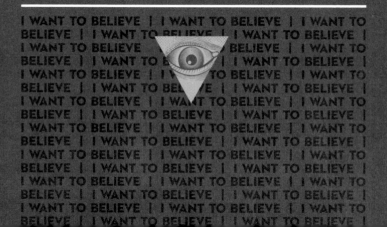

Who doesn't like a good secret? Or better yet, a good *conspiracy*—the secret plans that only a few people know about? Who doesn't want to connect the dots if the line goes from an all-seeing eye, through a bag of Doritos, and on to world domination and reptilian overlords?

You're reading this book, right? So you know I mean *you*!

Actually, I mean all of us. We *Homo sapiens* are a conspiracy-loving bunch of mammals. We were born this way: It *is* all in our heads.

# BLAME IT ON THE BRAIN

The human brain is a nonstop, information-gathering, sorting machine. That gray matter in our heads sucks up the energy of 20 percent of the calories we consume. The brain's nearly 100 billion neurons—its signaling cells—fire off hundreds of electrical pulses to one another every second. Why all the hubbub? To answer one question:

## "WHAT'S GOING ON?"

As you move through the world, your vast neuron network is making note of everything you experience. It sees everything as meaningful. Evolutionarily speaking, this is pretty handy: If you were an early human who didn't figure out danger, you'd end up as dinner!

THE SYMBOLICAL

ILLUSTRATING ALL THE

PHRENOLOGICAL DEVE

OF THE

HUMAN HE

Your brain rapidly sifts through its mental data bank. It's looking for patterns, connections, and cause and effect. Impressions become linked with each other and bingo: You're creating reality without even thinking about it—and you're doing it really fast!

Sometimes in the midst of all this hyperactivity, the brain will confuse details or create meaningless patterns.

## WATCH THIS:

**COINCIDENCES AND CONSPIRACIES
BOTH HAVE TWELVE LETTERS**

**THEY EACH HAVE FIVE VOWELS**

**THEY BOTH START WITH CO**

**TA-DA! COINCIDENCES = CONSPIRACIES**

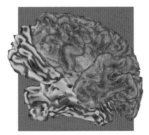

# YOUR POINT IS?

Whether or not you believe that conclusion about "coincidences equaling conspiracies" depends on your confirmation bias.

## SAY WHAT?

Translation: **Your brain doesn't like coincidences, inexplicable events, or things that don't add up. It seeks out meaning or motive no matter what. At the same time, your brain is filtering information based on what you already believe or know to be true. That's confirmation bias. When your brain gets new data, it confirms it against known data.**

We also like to think that stuff happens because someone *intended* it to happen. Don't know why or who that "someone" is? It doesn't really matter: "It is what it is."

And if something really big happens, then something or someone really big must be behind it, right?

All of this is partly why conspiracies like the Illuminati appeal to us. Your brain is begging, "I want to believe!"

# THE THING IS:
## THE ILLUMINATI IS REAL.

## GET YOUR CONSIPRACY ON

## THE ELEMENTS OF A GOOD CONSPIRACY ARE:

**QUESTIONS THAT HAVE
NO CLEAR ANSWERS**

▲

**COINCIDENCES
(ALWAYS CLAIM THERE IS NO SUCH THING!)**

▲

**THINGS THAT AREN'T WHAT THEY SEEM TO BE—
JUST TACK ON " . . . *OR IS IT?* "**

▲

**"THEY."
THE POWERFUL PEOPLE BEHIND THE SCENES
WHO CAN PULL OFF ABSOLUTELY ANYTHING.**

SHINE A LIGHT | SHINE A LIGHT | SHINE A LIGHT |
SHINE A LIGHT | SHINE A LIGHT | SHINE A LIGHT | SHINE
A LIGHT | SHINE A LIGHT | SHINE A LIGHT | SHINE A
LIGHT | SHINE A LIGHT | SHINE A LIGHT | SHINE A LIGHT
| SHINE A LIGHT | SHINE A LIGHT | SHINE A LIGHT |
SHINE A LIGHT | SHINE A LIGHT | SHINE A LIGHT | SHINE
A LIGHT | SHINE A LIGHT | SHINE A LIGHT | SHINE A
LIGHT | SHINE A LIGHT | SHINE A LIGHT | SHINE A LIGHT
| SHINE A LIGHT | SHINE A LIGHT | SHINE A LIGHT |
SHINE A LIGHT | SHINE A LIGHT | SHINE A LIGHT | SHINE
A LIGHT | SHINE A LIGHT | SHINE A LIGHT | SHINE A
LIGHT | SHINE A LIGHT | SHINE A LIGHT | SHINE A LIGHT
| SHINE A LIGHT | SHINE A LIGHT | SHINE A LIGHT |
SHINE A LIGHT | SHINE A LIGHT | SHINE A LIGHT | SHINE
A LIGHT | SHINE A LIGHT | SHINE A LIGHT | SHINE A
LIGHT | SHINE A LIGHT | SHINE A LIGHT | SHINE A LIGHT |

# SHINE A LIGHT

SHINE A LIGHT | SHINE A LIGHT | SHINE A LIGHT | SHINE
A LIGHT | SHINE A LIGHT | SHINE A LIGHT | SHINE A
LIGHT | SHINE A LIGHT | SHINE A LIGHT | SHINE A LIGHT
| SHINE A LIGHT | SHINE A LIGHT | SHINE A LIGHT |
SHINE A LIGHT | SHINE A LIGHT | SHINE A LIGHT | SHINE
A LIGHT | SHINE A LIGHT | SHINE A LIGHT | SHINE A
LIGHT | SHINE A LIGHT | SHINE A LIGHT | SHINE A LIGHT
| SHINE A LIGHT | SHINE A LIGHT | SHINE A LIGHT |
SHINE A LIGHT | SHINE A LIGHT | SHINE A LIGHT | SHINE
A LIGHT | SHINE A LIGHT | SHINE A LIGHT | SHINE A
LIGHT | SHINE A LIGHT | SHINE A LIGHT | SHINE A LIGHT
| SHINE A LIGHT | SHINE A LIGHT | SHINE A LIGHT |
SHINE A LIGHT | SHINE A LIGHT | SHINE A LIGHT | SHINE
A LIGHT | SHINE A LIGHT | SHINE A LIGHT | SHINE A
LIGHT | SHINE A LIGHT | SHINE A LIGHT | SHINE A LIGHT
| SHINE A LIGHT | SHINE A LIGHT | SHINE A LIGHT |
SHINE A LIGHT | SHINE A LIGHT | SHINE A LIGHT | SHINE

On May 1, 1776, five men met by torchlight deep in a forest in Europe. One of them had a brilliant idea: Let's start a secret club.

Behold, the Illuminati!

The big thinker in the woods was Adam Weishaupt, a dean at the University of Ingolstadt in Bavaria. This was a conservative and Catholic region of the southern part of what is now modern Germany.

Weishaupt scorned the narrow-minded thinking all around him. He and his secret club were on a mission: Save the world from superstition and ignorance! They called themselves the Perfectibilists. (Go big or go home.)

ADAM WEISHAUPT (1748-1811*) AND HIS DEATH MASK—
BECAUSE IT'S CREEPY AND WE CAN!

*SOME SOURCES SAY 1830.
*EVERYTHING'S* A MYSTERY WITH THIS GUY.

The eighteenth century was the Age of Enlightenment. Intellectuals like Weishaupt studied philosophy and science. They weren't looking to royal and religious rulers for answers. Weishaupt and his pals were radical thinkers who believed people would only be happy when they were free of the powerful, self-serving leaders who kept the majority of folks poor and ignorant. Their intentions were noble and enlightened: Free the sheeple!

Weishaupt changed the name of the Perfectibilists to the Order of the Illuminati, which means "the enlightened ones" in Latin.

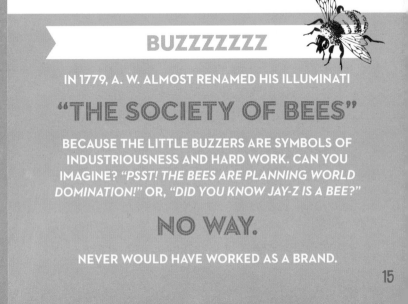

## BUZZZZZZ

IN 1779, A. W. ALMOST RENAMED HIS ILLUMINATI

# "THE SOCIETY OF BEES"

BECAUSE THE LITTLE BUZZERS ARE SYMBOLS OF INDUSTRIOUSNESS AND HARD WORK. CAN YOU IMAGINE? *"PSST! THE BEES ARE PLANNING WORLD DOMINATION!"* OR, *"DID YOU KNOW JAY-Z IS A BEE?"*

## NO WAY.

NEVER WOULD HAVE WORKED AS A BRAND.

# WHO MADE *YOU* THE ENLIGHTENED ONES?

Adam Weishaupt and his Order of the Illuminati weren't the only enlightened folks around. In eighteenth-century Europe, there was a whole movement of big ideas about big ideas. There was a lot of thinking going on in this Age of Enlightenment. #daretoknow (Okay, the guy who used that phrase would have written it with pen and ink and in Latin—*sapere aude*—but always good to have a motto, right?)

Enlightenment thinkers were all about being clued in. They studied the world around them and questioned who should be in charge of it. (Hint: The answer is *not* a king or a pope.) These European intellectuals promoted new ideas about freedom of speech, individual liberty, and democracy. (Can you see where this is heading?)

The Age of Enlightenment is also called the Age of Reason because it was a time when questioning traditions and actually proving ideas replaced just accepting whatever you were told. Enlightened ones believed that individuals had a right to be free and happy. That governments should only exist to make life better for citizens. That people could live fuller lives by seeking knowledge and experience. That freedom of thought and expression were essential.

## DANGEROUS IDEAS!

Clearly the people with political power and the church leaders did not want their authority challenged. Throughout the Enlightenment, people were punished for spreading bold new ideas. But the Enlightenment brought about reform, too—and sometimes revolution, as in American and French.

Weishaupt called dibs on the Illuminati name, but plenty of other people were also shining a light on how things should work. Ideas from the Enlightenment shaped modern politics, economics, education, and culture. And oh yeah, the whole idea of the United States.

# HEAVYWEIGHTS OF THE
# ENLIGHTENMENT

*BEING ALL EQUAL AND INDEPENDENT, NO ONE OUGHT TO HARM ANOTHER IN HIS LIFE, HEALTH, LIBERTY, OR POSSESSIONS.*

John Locke (1632–1704), an English philosopher and doctor, was one of the most famous names of the Enlightenment. Among his many influential ideas is that people are free and equal and they should decide what form of government they want. This was revolutionary at a time when kings and queens ruled nearly every corner of the earth!

*THERE ARE THREE PRINCIPAL MEANS OF ACQUIRING KNOWLEDGE... OBSERVATION OF NATURE, REFLECTION, AND EXPERIMENTATION.*

Denis Diderot (1713–1784). This French philosopher and 150 of his pals created a mammoth thirty-five-volume encyclopedia of all the world's knowledge. Word!

> *WE HOLD THESE TRUTHS TO BE SELF-EVIDENT, THAT ALL MEN ARE CREATED EQUAL, THAT THEY ARE ENDOWED BY THEIR CREATOR WITH CERTAIN UNALIENABLE RIGHTS, THAT AMONG THESE ARE LIFE, LIBERTY, AND THE PURSUIT OF HAPPINESS.*

Thomas Jefferson (1743–1826), like the other Founding Fathers, was inspired by Enlightenment ideas, especially the ones about human rights, the responsibilities of government, and the value of science. Jefferson was the main author of the Declaration of Independence and the second vice president and third president of the United States. He was also an architect, lawyer, farmer, and inventor.

> *VIRTUE CAN ONLY FLOURISH AMONG EQUALS.*

Mary Wollstonecraft (1759–1797) was an English writer and philosopher with a truly enlightened idea: Let's educate women! She explained her ideas in her book *A Vindication of the Rights of Woman.* Many people consider her the mother of feminism.

# THE MAN BEHIND THE LEGEND

So who exactly was Adam Weishaupt, founder of ~~the Perfectibilists~~, ~~the Society of Bees~~, the Order of the Illuminati?

"An unpractical bookworm without necessary experience in the world," according to one eighteenth-century writer. OUCH!

Actually, it's true that Weishaupt had a pretty quiet life at first. He was born in Bavaria in 1748. When he was five years old, his father died. Adam went to live with his godfather, Johann Adam Ickstatt (awesome last name, right?).

Some cool things about the godfather: He was a baron, and he had a huge library with a lot of books… *banned* books. It turns out that Ickstatt was enlightened!

## BANNED BOOKS

### 1700s
*AN ESSAY CONCERNING HUMAN UNDERSTANDING*
by JOHN LOCKE

DIDEROT'S *ENCYCLOPÉDIE*
(THAT COUNTS AS THIRTY-FIVE BOOKS!)

### 2000s
HARRY POTTER SERIES
by J. K. ROWLING

CAPTAIN UNDERPANTS SERIES
by DAV PILKEY

Adam was educated by the Jesuits, an order of Catholic priests. The Jesuits were not very big on questioning authority. Luckily, young Adam spent hours in his godfather's library. He soaked up all kinds of radical ideas.

Adam Weishaupt eventually earned a law degree, got married, and became dean of law at the University of Ingolstadt. This only angered the Jesuits: That job usually went to one of them! Professor Weishaupt used his position to spread his enlightened ideas about how to improve society.

Weishaupt decided to go underground—more like into the woods, actually—with all his rationalist thinking. He formed his secret group and the rest is history ... or *mystery*!

Spoiler alert: Adam Weishaupt's plan for a glorious secret society didn't remain a secret. In 1785, he was banished from Bavaria. He wrote about why the Illuminati was a good idea.

He always kept an all-seeing eye open for Bavarian agents who might want to assassinate him.

The Bavarian Illuminati were a secretive bunch right from the get-go. Weishaupt's first rule was: "Let it [the Illuminati] never appear in any place in its own name, but always covered by another name, and another occupation." He wanted another club's name to hide behind.

So he decided to "illuminize" the Freemasons.

The Freemasons (or Masons) were a respectable sort of do-good, back your bros, men's club (which they still are). They were exactly what Weishaupt needed to help build Illuminati membership on the sly. In 1777, our man A. W. became a member of a Masonic lodge in Munich and started working from within.

A fellow Mason, Baron Adolf Franz Friedrich, Freiherr von Knigge, joined Weishaupt and his Illuminati in 1780. Knigge was well connected and good at recruiting. He brought in some "name" members like Prince Ferdinand, Duke of Brunswick, and the famous German writer Johann Wolfgang von Goethe.

The Illuminati, now a secret society within a secret society, spread across Germany, Austria, France, Italy, Hungary, and Switzerland. By 1784, membership was said to be almost three thousand. Illuminati infiltrated Masonic lodges. They held positions of power and authority in governments and other institutions. But they were always "covered by another name."

ADOLF FRANZ FRIEDRICH, FREIHERR VON KNIGGE (1752-1796) WENT FROM MR. SECRET SOCIETY TO MR. NICE GUY. IN GERMANY, THE BARON IS FAMOUS FOR A BOOK HE WROTE ON MANNERS AND GOOD BEHAVIOR. ONE OF HIS RULES? "LEARN TO TAKE ON THE TONE OF WHATEVER COMPANY YOU FIND YOURSELF IN." *SOOOO* ILLUMINATI!

# YOU SAY MASON, I SAY FREEMASON

The Illuminati were secretive, but there was an actual beginning to their story. The Freemasons were more well-known, but had very murky origins. Did they really build the Temple of Solomon in the tenth century BCE? Are they linked to the legendary Knights Templar? Did they start as a medieval guild of stoneworkers who built the great cathedrals of Europe? Nobody knows for sure. There are even different accounts of when or why "Freemason" versus "Mason" is used—or if it even matters.

The *recorded* history of organized freemasonry starts in London, England, in 1717. Four different groups of men met together in a tavern: brews, bros, and bam! You have the first Grand Lodge of Masons.

A *mason* is someone who builds with stone, brick, or tile. The word *freemason* probably came from the skilled medieval masons who worked with freestone, a type of soft rock that can be carved into beautiful and very detailed shapes.

Freemasons belong to local groups called *lodges*. Originally, lodge members were actual stonecutters. They were the ones who most likely developed the passwords and secret handshakes. Most medieval Masons couldn't read, so they weren't carrying around résumés when they moved from place to place building castles and cathedrals. A secret word or special grip would identify them as experienced masons to their boss on a new job.

Eventually, the Freemasons started letting non-stonecutters into the club. These "adopted" Masons really went all in for the secret symbols and rituals.

All Masons made a point of keeping the *cowans*—their name for non-Masons—in the dark. Especially any snoops who might be trying to uncover their secrets.

## RESTING STONE FACE

FREEMASONS SOMETIMES GOT FREAKY WITH THEIR CARVINGS, ESPECIALLY ON CATHEDRALS.

The Knights Templar was a religious society formed in 1119. They were the defenders of the Kingdom of Jerusalem in the Middle East. They were also bodyguards for European Christians traveling there, who were known as *pilgrims.*

The Christian king of Jerusalem welcomed them to set up headquarters at his palace on the Temple Mount—which was right near the ancient ruins of the Temple of Solomon. (Yup, the same place those Freemasons supposedly built.)

The Knights called themselves the Poor Fellow-Soldiers of Christ and of the Temple of Solomon. All the "temple" this, "temple" that led to the shorter name: Knights Templar. (Plus, the knights weren't exactly poor after a while.)

Grateful pilgrims and other Christians donated money and land to the Knights. The Knights Templar amassed fortunes, invested in real estate, built castles, and owned a fleet of ships used for trading.

They also set up one of the first banking systems. (Bonus: They didn't have to pay taxes because they were a charity!) Traveling pilgrims deposited their riches with a local Templar, got a receipt, then headed off on their journey. When they arrived safely in Jerusalem, they presented the receipt to the Templars there and received an equal amount of riches. All for a fee to the Templars, of course.

The Knights lent money to kings, queens, and other royalty, and became pretty rich and powerful. This didn't sit so well with people like King Philip IV of France (who owed them money) and Pope Clement V (who owed his job to King Philip).

On October 13, 1307, Templars across Europe were rounded up. They were accused of crimes against the Catholic Church and all kinds of evildoing. Knights were tortured and their fortunes seized. Some Templar leaders were burned at the stake!

But according to legend, a few of the Knights

escaped to Scotland on treasure-laden ships. By the eighteenth century, some Freemasons wove that story into the history of their own group. They claimed that the Freemasons were descended from the Knights Templars who had made it to Scotland.

But that is a very weak link, and an even weaker one to the Illuminati.

Rumors swirled for centuries that the Knights had discovered secret treasure by digging in the ruins of the Temple of Solomon. That the Templars found the Holy Grail *and* the Ark of the Covenant. (Tough luck, Indiana Jones!)

There's no proof, of course, but the rumors are fuel for some pretty good stories. Just Google Dan Brown.

FREEMASONS GET FUNKY!

In the early 1700s, it was dangerous to talk openly about freedom, democracy, or scientific breakthroughs that challenged tradition. Authorities came down hard when they discovered people spreading revolutionary ideas. That's why groups like the Freemasons and the Illuminati were secret societies. If you held enlightened ideas, it was best to avoid the spotlight.

# WAG YOUR TONGUE AND YOUR HEAD MIGHT ROLL.

To protect themselves, Freemasons took vows of secrecy and did not reveal what took place in their meetings. This is still true. It's also true that most lodges don't allow discussions about organized religion, politics, or political parties. Spiritual enlightenment is a big part of the Masonic mission. So is self-improvement, doing good in the world, and helping your fellow Freemasons.

Beyond that, figuring out Freemasonry is really complicated. There's no single set of rules and rituals that every Mason follows. There's no grand pooh-bah who is in charge of every Masonic lodge in the world. And no Freemason is ever going to spill the beans.

## YOU'RE IN, *MAN!*

MASONIC LODGES HAVE PRETTY OPEN ADMISSIONS POLICIES—UNLESS YOU HAPPEN TO BE FEMALE. FREEMASONS ARE A *FRATERNAL* ORGANIZATION, WHICH MEANS ONLY MEN CAN JOIN. BUT IF YOU'RE A MAN OF GOOD CHARACTER WHO BELIEVES IN A SUPREME BEING, THEN "WELCOME, BROTHER."

# THE THIRD DEGREE

Lots of people think Freemasons are some kind of spooky cult. They're wrong: Freemasons are all about the "rite."

A Masonic rite is a degree—or level—of membership. Different branches of Freemasons have different rites. There can be thousands of variations. But they're all built on a system of three essential degrees: Entered Apprentice, Fellowcraft (or Journeyman), and Master Mason. (*Pssst!* The secret passwords for each are "Boaz," "Jachin," and "Mahabone.")

Initiation might involve being blindfolded, reading and listening to lectures, or putting on plays. The goal is to study and work your way through each of the degrees.

A BLINDFOLDED FRENCH DUDE IS ABOUT TO BECOME AN APPRENTICE FREEMASON DURING THE 1800S. *OO-LA-LA!*

New Masons get something special to wear to show they're in the club: a white apron! (Just like the ones medieval stonecutters wore.) As you move up in degrees, you get to add fancy gold trim and embroidered symbols to your apron.

THIS MASONIC APRON BELONGED TO MERIWETHER LEWIS—YES, *THAT* LEWIS, AS IN THE FAMOUS LEWIS AND CLARK EXPEDITION.

Have you ever watched a crime show where the suspect is peppered with questions and gets "the third degree" to make him talk? That phrase comes from the Freemasons! You have to pass a tough examination to be awarded your Masonic third degree.

Freemasons believe the universe was created by a divine Great Architect, and that studying geometry and architecture will help us to understand it. (Makes sense, right? We're talking about a group formed by builders!)

Masonic learning is based on symbols and *allegory*—stories, poems, or pictures that are meant to represent a certain idea. Freemasons love their illuminating images and hidden layers! And since they came from a long line of stonecutters, tools like squares, compasses, ladders, or trowels are all big-time symbols for them. So is a black-and-white checkered floor, a tile pattern that stands for the good and evil of human life. Heavy!

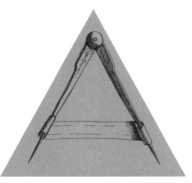

**A MASONIC TRACING BOARD**

Keeping track of all these secret meanings and memorizing them for the Masonic degree quiz is a lot of work! Luckily, there's a kind of Freemason cheat sheet called a tracing board. Mentors can use these boards to review symbols and meanings with members of lower degrees.

# PYRAMID SCHEME

*Meanwhile, back inside the Illuminati . . .*

The original Bavarian Illuminati was organized as a pyramid. (Naturally!) And, naturally, founder Adam Weishaupt was at the top. He gave himself the title "Illuminatus Rex," meaning "the Illuminated King"—even though the I-mission was freedom from monarchs! Two people were under him, then two under each of them, etc. Information was shared on a need-to-know basis, which was supposed to protect the group's secrecy. Nobody except A. W. ever completely knew what was going on.

Illuminati membership was by invitation only. "Insinuators" scoped out likely recruits. Male? Good family name? Wealthy? Let's talk. Over thirty-five? Sorry, you're probably too old for enlightened thinking.

Once you joined, you were ordered around by "Unknown Superiors." Illuminati

"Scrutators" spied on you, writing down everything you did or said. If your notes didn't match up with their notes, you were out. (On the plus side, if you made it near the top, you got a uniform, a red cap, and a shepherd's crook. Woo-hoo!)

**A SHEPHERD'S CROOK**

*You* took vows of loyalty and silence about the Illuminati. *They* knew everything about you, which guaranteed you'd stay quiet.

## INSINUATORS, SUPERIORS, AND SCRUTATORS—OH MY!

# THE NURSERY

Illuminatus Rex Weishaupt proclaimed, "We cannot use people as they are, but begin by making them over." Sure, the Illuminati were all for freethinking. But if you wanted to be one of them, you had to get with the program... *their* program!

Like the Freemasons, the Illuminati had different levels of membership. Working through these levels was a cross between school and a cult: endless note-taking, journal-keeping, detailed book reports on everything you read, and any of your bad habits, right down to how you slept.

Originally, there were three major Illuminati levels—

## THE NURSERY,

## THE MASONRY,

## AND THE MYSTERIES.

For Baron von Knigge, who was a much more mystical kind of guy than Weishaupt, that just wasn't enough. More rites! More rituals!

## GET OUT OF THE NURSERY

## TO-DO LIST

△

*MAKE A LIST OF EVERY BOOK YOU OWN*

△

*MAKE A LIST OF ALL YOUR ENEMIES*

△

*READ THE BIBLE*

△

*READ THE CLASSICS BY GREEK AND ROMAN PHILOSOPHERS*

△

*READ CONFUCIUS, THE CHINESE PHILOSOPHER, WHILE YOU'RE AT IT*

△

*WRITE ABOUT YOUR FAMILY: WHAT THEY LIKE, WHAT THEY DO, HOW MUCH MONEY THEY HAVE, AND DON'T FORGET TO LIST THEIR WEAKNESSES*

△

*NOW DO THE SAME THING ABOUT ANYBODY YOU MEET*

△

*KEEP TRACK OF YOUR REACTIONS TO CURRENT EVENTS*

△

*SPY ON EVERYBODY . . . AND REPORT BACK!*

# ON THE LEVEL

Remember: Adam Weishaupt and Baron von Knigge were both Masons. This influenced how they developed the Illuminati levels. So did A. W.'s Jesuit education. He was the one who was so strict about all the rules.

## THE NURSERY

*NOVICE: See the to-do list on page 39*

*MINERVAL: Named after Minerva, the Roman goddess of wisdom*

*ILLUMINATUS MINOR (OR MASTER): Secret password is Nosce te ipsum (Know thyself)*

**OF COURSE, MINERVA HERSELF COULD NOT HAVE JOINED THE ORDER OF THE ILLUMINATI OR THE FREEMASONS: NO GIRLS ALLOWED!**

# THE MASONRY

*APPRENTICE*

*COMPANION*

*MASTER: Who wouldn't want
to earn this title?*

# THE MYSTERIES

*PRIEST: Weird title for a group that didn't like
organized religion, right?*

*PRINCE: Please be advised: initiation will include
blindfolding*

*MAGUS: A fancy word for a smart person or a
magician. Things get sketchy here . . . The Bavarian
Illuminati didn't last long enough to get all the rituals
written up*

*KING: Only one spot open here, and it's taken!*

# DEATH TO THE ENLIGHTENED ONES!

Surveillance; secrecy; radical, enlightened ideas: Do you smell conspiracy? Well, the Bavarian authorities certainly did.

By 1785, the Illuminati were banned in Bavaria. Members were arrested. Authorities claimed they found notes on counterfeiting, fake wax seals, recipes for invisible ink and poison, instructions for a build-your-own "infernal machine"—a box to hold your secret stuff that explodes in the wrong hands—and (the horror!) plans for a female branch. These things were clearly proof positive that the Illuminati were plotting against the government and the Catholic Church, *right*?

Two years later, the Bavarians banned *all* secret societies. If you were identified as an Illuminati or caught recruiting, you'd be "deprived of life by the sword." Weishaupt kept his head and fled to another part of Germany. His order disbanded.

The real Illuminati lasted from 1776 to 1787, or for the same eleven years between the Declaration of Independence and the proposal of the US Constitution. Don't get all woo-woo on this: The American Founding Fathers were enlightened, too. *Illuminism* (enlightened thinking) was in the air … and to the conspiracy-minded, the Illuminati had just gone underground.

## THE FACE ON THE
## DOLLAR BILL

**ADAM WEISHAUPT CONTINUED TO WRITE ABOUT ILLUMINISM UNTIL HE DIED IN 1811 … *OR DID HE?***

**A POPULAR NOVEL FROM THE 1970s SAID THAT HE FLED TO AMERICA; KIDNAPPED, KILLED, AND IMPERSONATED GEORGE WASHINGTON; SECRETLY SERVED AS THE FIRST PRESIDENT OF THE UNITED STATES; AND THEN PUT HIS OWN FACE ON THE DOLLAR BILL.**

## BUT NOVELS ARE ONLY FICTION, *AREN'T THEY?*

SECRET SIGNS | SECRET SIGNS | SECRET SIGNS |
SIGNS | SECRET SIGNS | SECRET SIGNS | SECRET SIGNS
| SECRET SIGNS | SECRET SIGNS | SECRET SIGNS |
SECRET SIGNS | SECRET SIGNS | SECRET SIGNS | SECRET
SIGNS | SECRET SIGNS | SECRET SIGNS | SECRET SIGNS
| SECRET SIGNS | SECRET SIGNS | SECRET SIGNS |
SECRET SIGNS | SECRET SIGNS | SECRET SIGNS | SECRET
SIGNS | SECRET SIGNS | SECRET SIGNS | SECRET SIGNS
| SECRET SIGNS | SECRET SIGNS | SECRET SIGNS |
SECRET SIGNS | SECRET SIGNS | SECRET SIGNS | SECRET
SIGNS | SECRET SIGNS | SECRET SIGNS | SECRET SIGNS
| SECRET SIGNS | SECRET SIGNS | SECRET SIGNS |

# SECRET
# SIGNS

SECRET SIGNS | SECRET SIGNS | SECRET SIGNS | SECRET
SIGNS | SECRET SIGNS | SECRET SIGNS | SECRET SIGNS |
SECRET SIGNS | SECRE          SECRET SIGNS | SECRET
SIGNS | SECRET SIGNS          SIGNS | SECRET SIGNS |
SECRET SIGNS | SECRET S       SECRET SIGNS | SECRET
SIGNS | SECRET SIGNS | S       RET SIGNS | SECRET SIGNS
| SECRET SIGNS | SECRET SIGNS | SECRET SIGNS |
SECRET SIGNS | SECRET SIGNS | SECRET SIGNS | SECRET
SIGNS | SECRET SIGNS | SECRET SIGNS | SECRET SIGNS |
SECRET SIGNS | SECRET SIGNS | SECRET SIGNS | SECRET
SIGNS | SECRET SIGNS | SECRET SIGNS | SECRET SIGNS |
SECRET SIGNS | SECRET SIGNS | SECRET SIGNS | SECRET
SIGNS | SECRET SIGNS | SECRET SIGNS | SECRET SIGNS |
SECRET SIGNS | SECRET SIGNS | SECRET SIGNS | SECRET
SIGNS | SECRET SIGNS | SECRET SIGNS | SECRET SIGNS |

The Order of the Illuminati has been a hot topic for almost 250 years. Now, that's some unending trending! And if there's one thing that keeps people talking about you, it's wondering about the secrets you may be keeping. Adam Weishaupt and his Bavarian Illuminati were all in.

# CODE NAME:
## ANYTHING *BUT* "ILLUMINATI"

△ *DON'T SPELL OUT I_ _ _ _ _ _ _ _,
JUST DRAW THIS:*

△ *WRITE IN CODE,
AND DON'T SIGN YOUR REAL NAME.*

△ *DATE STUFF USING THE PERSIAN CALENDAR.
START COUNTING FROM THE YEAR 630. SLY!*

△ *THERE ARE GOING TO BE
A LOT OF PASSWORDS.
HOPE YOU KNOW LATIN!*

△ *LEARN TO WRITE WITH BOTH
YOUR RIGHT AND LEFT HANDS. SNEAKY!*
*(IN THIS TOP SECRET GROUP, THE LEFT HAND DOESN'T
KNOW WHAT THE RIGHT HAND IS DOING!)*

△ *WRITE IN INVISIBLE INK.*

# HOW TO MAKE

## INVISIBLE INK

THE ILLUMINATI DIDN'T PUBLISH THEIR RECIPE FOR INVISIBLE INK, SO WE DON'T KNOW EXACTLY HOW THEY MADE IT. BUT HERE'S HOW YOU CAN DO IT:

---

*SQUEEZE LEMON JUICE INTO A BOWL*

*ADD A FEW DROPS OF WATER AND STIR*

*DIP A Q-TIP INTO THE MIXTURE*

*WRITE AN ENLIGHTENING MESSAGE ON A PIECE OF PAPER*

*WHEN THE PAPER DRIES, HOLD IT UP TO A LIGHTBULB*

*NOTE:* DON'T TRY THIS WITH YOUR HOMEWORK!

# CODE WRITING

Secret societies have stuff they want to keep secret. DUH! But members have to know what's what. So groups like the Knights Templar, the Freemasons, and the Order of the Illuminati used ciphers. Ciphers are codes that can be used to encrypt—or hide—a message.

One popular cipher is the Pigpen. (Real pigpens are divided into sections to keep pigs from fighting and to keep piglets safe.) The Pigpen is also called the Masonic cipher because it was used so often by Freemasons and their secret brothers, the Illuminati. They used it to write messages even from beyond the grave! You can find Pigpen code, along with other symbols, on some Masonic tombstones.

# HERE'S A WIDELY USED PIGPEN CIPHER.

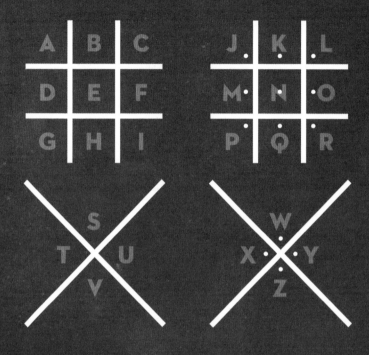

**NEXT TIME YOU NEED TO SEND A SECRET MESSAGE OR CREATE A SUPERCOOL T-SHIRT, GO FOR IT!**

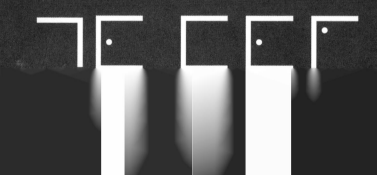

# CLASSIC SYMBOLS

The Illuminati borrowed the all-seeing eye symbol from the Freemasons, who scooped it from the ancient Egyptians. The eye of the Egyptian sun god Ra became an all-purpose flying eyeball signifying power, protection, and a supreme being keeping an eye on you!

The pyramid is another borrow from the Egyptians—history's most famous pyramid builders—via the Freemasons. Its horizontal layers represent the different Illuminati ranks. You can see it's a structure with fewer stones at the top, and a lot more at the bottom. That worked just fine for top banana (or stone!) Illuminatus Rex Weishaupt.

To the Freemasons, the pyramid symbolized the Great Architect of the Universe. That is how they described the divine supreme being who created the world.

The owl is the sign of Minerva, the Roman goddess of wisdom. Illuminati initiates into the Minerval level had to recite a long poem about an owl. They also wore owl medals like the one above from a pamphlet published by the Illuminati in 1788.

The Bavarian Illuminati may have had a secret handshake—press my hand three times with your thumb and I know we're I-brothers. They took their signs and symbols seriously. They weren't shooting devil horns or triangles at each other! They were forward thinkers who were into learning and the classics—the ancient texts and art where they found most of their symbolism. They definitely weren't doodling monarch butterflies and triangle stars or any other so-called Illuminati signs all over their notebooks.

Of course they did have that invisible ink…

Although the Illuminati and the Freemasons were secret groups that wanted to stay hidden, they definitely went in for branding. They had name recognition, slogans ("Know thyself"), and logos (that all-seeing eye!).

You can build your own secret society brand. Just follow these few easy steps:

## PICK A NAME THAT SAYS *POWERFUL, IMPORTANT,* AND *MYSTERIOUS.*

Check out a thesaurus for words that mean *powerful, important, mysterious.* Add a fun noun that starts with the same letter, like the Mystifying Monkeys. Always add *the* so your club sounds like the one and only. If it's going to be secret, you want it to sound exclusive, too.

### *(AVOID GOOFY LABELS LIKE THE ALMIGHTY OOMPA-LOOMPAS.)*

# CHOOSE A LATIN MOTTO AS YOUR SLOGAN

This will make you sound really smart—and fool people who don't know Latin. Some suggestions:

*Carpe diem* = Seize the day. (Or go with *carpe noctem*—seize the night—if you're not a morning person.)

*Corvus oculum corvi non eruit* = A crow will not pluck out the eye of another crow. (Gruesome, but gets the message across: Members of your club take care of each other.)

*Velocius quam asparagi coquantur* = Faster than cooking asparagus (No one will know what the heck you mean here, so it's a good choice for a very, very secret society.)

# GO WITH A BASIC GEOMETRIC SHAPE FOR A LOGO

Triangles are overused. How about a nice rhombus, polygon, or trapezoid? Or did you know *kite* is a geometric shape? Sweet.

Whatever you choose, put a big, wide-open eye inside it.

WHODUNIT HISTORY | WHODUNIT HISTORY | WHODUNIT
HISTORY | WHODUNIT HISTORY | WHODUNIT HISTORY |
WHODUNIT HISTORY | WHODUNIT HISTORY | WHODUNIT
HISTORY | WHODUNIT HISTORY | WHODUNIT HISTORY
| WHODUNIT HISTORY | WHODUNIT HISTORY | WHODUNIT
HISTORY | WHODUNIT HISTORY | WHODUNIT HISTORY |
WHODUNIT HISTORY | WHODUNIT HISTORY | WHODUNIT
HISTORY | WHODUNIT HISTORY | WHODUNIT HISTORY
| WHODUNIT HISTORY | WHODUNIT HISTORY | WHODUNIT
HISTORY | WHODUNIT HISTORY | WHODUNIT HISTORY |
WHODUNIT HISTORY | WHODUNIT HISTORY | WHODUNIT
HISTORY | WHODUNIT HISTORY | WHODUNIT HISTORY
| WHODUNIT HISTORY | WHODUNIT HISTORY | WHODUNIT
HISTORY | WHODUNIT HISTORY | WHODUNIT HISTORY |
WHODUNIT HISTORY | WHODUNIT HISTORY | WHODUNIT

# WHODUNIT
# HISTORY

WHODUNIT HISTORY | WHODUNIT HISTORY | WHODUNIT
HISTORY | WHODUNIT HISTORY | WHODUNIT HISTORY |
WHODUNIT HISTORY | WHODUNIT HISTORY | WHODUNIT
HISTORY | WHODUNIT HISTORY | WHODUNIT HISTORY |
WHODUNIT HISTORY | WHODUNIT HISTORY | WHODUNIT
HISTORY | WHODUNIT HISTORY | WHODUNIT HISTORY |
WHODUNIT HISTORY | WHODUNIT HISTORY | WHODUNIT
HISTORY | WHODUNIT HISTORY | WHODUNIT HISTORY
| WHODUNIT HISTORY | WHODUNIT HISTORY | WHODUNIT
HISTORY | WHODUNIT HISTORY | WHODUNIT HISTORY |
WHODUNIT HISTORY | WHODUNIT HISTORY | WHODUNIT
HISTORY | WHODUNIT HISTORY | WHODUNIT HISTORY |
WHODUNIT HISTORY | WHODUNIT HISTORY | WHODUNIT
HISTORY | WHODUNIT HISTORY | WHODUNIT HISTORY

Who hosted the Boston Tea Party?

Who revved up the French Revolution?

Who told the British to torch the
White House in 1814?

Hint: The answer starts and ends with an *I*
(according to some folks).

There are more than two million #Illuminati posts on Instagram. Google *Illuminati* and you'll get nearly fifty-four *million* site pages. But interestingly enough, the group rates only a couple of pages in most serious books and articles about secret societies. And those entries are about the Bavarian Illuminati, which we know lasted a total of eleven years... *or did it?*

The big *I* was barely banned and scattered before writers like French Jesuit priest Abbé Augustin Barruel and Scottish physicist and mathematician John Robison cranked out eighteenth-century best sellers that kept the whole Illuminati conspiracy idea alive.

# FAKE NEWS AND CONSPIRACIES ALWAYS SELL!

# PROOFS
### OF A
# CONSPIRACY
#### AGAINST ALL THE
### *RELIGIONS AND GOVERNMENTS*
#### OF
# EUROPE,
#### CARRIED ON
#### IN THE SECRET MEETINGS
#### OF
### *FREE MASONS, ILLUMINATI,*
#### AND
### *READING SOCIETIES.*
#### COLLECTED FROM GOOD AUTHORITIES,
### BY JOHN ROBISON, A. M.

PROFESSOR OF NATURAL PHILOSOPHY, AND SECRETARY TO THE
ROYAL SOCIETY OF EDINBURGH.

*Nam tua res agitur paries cum proximus ardet.*

THE FOURTH EDITION.

TO WHICH IS ADDED, A POSTSCRIPT.

---

"BY DESTROYING THE [ILLUMINATI] PAPERS, ALL OPPORTUNITY WAS LOST FOR AUTHENTICATING THE INNOCENCE AND USEFULNESS OF THE ORDER."

**TRANSLATION:**
*I* COULD BE LYING, BUT *YOU'LL* NEVER PROVE IT.

---

# MEMOIRS,

Illustrating the

# *HISTORY of JACOBINISM,*

Written in FRENCH by

### THE ABBÉ BARRUEL,

And translated into ENGLISH by

### *THE HON. ROBERT CLIFFORD, F.R S. & A.S.*

Princes and Nations shall disappear from the face of the Earth . . . and this
REVOLUTION shall be the WORK OF SECRET SOCIETIES.
*Weishaupt's Discourse for the Mysteries.*

### *PART III.*

### *THE ANTISOCIAL CONSPIRACY.*

Second Edition, revised and corrected.

---

"... CONTAIN[S] IRREFRAGABLE PROOFS OF THE MOST DETESTABLE CONSPIRACY."

**TRANSLATION:**
I GOT THE GOODS ON THE ILLUMINATI AND I'M GONNA LET LOOSE.

Freemasonry arrived in the American colonies around 1730. The first Masonic lodge in America was founded in Philadelphia thirteen years after the Masons first organized in London. Benjamin Franklin joined a lodge in 1731 and was the Grand Master of Pennsylvania. George Washington was initiated at Lodge No. 4 in Fredericksburg, Virginia, in 1752.

BENJAMIN FRANKLIN (1706-1790) LOOKING FINE IN HIS MASONIC APRON. THE APRON WAS BASED ON THE WORK APRON STONEMASONS WORE IN THE 1600s AND 1700s.

GEORGE WASHINGTON (1732-1799) RECEIVED A COPY OF JOHN ROBISON'S CONSPIRACY BOOK. SO HE KEPT AN ALL-SEEING EYE OPEN FOR ANY ILLUMINATI WHO MIGHT BE TRYING TO SNEAK INTO THE AMERICAN MASONS.

Washington, Franklin, and some of America's other Founding Fathers were Masons. So were leading patriots like Paul Revere and John Hancock. But there is no proof that the Illuminati staged the Boston Tea Party in 1773, even though some of the colonists whooping it up onboard *were* Masons. (We see you, Paul Revere!) Ditto for the American Revolution. Not an Illuminati plot.

Yup, the Bavarian Illuminati did infiltrate Masonic lodges in France. Nope, they didn't buy up all the wheat in France so starving peasants would revolt, kill the royals, and then let the Illuminati take over. The French Revolution was sparked by new, enlightened ideas about equality and the desperation of overtaxed, underfed poor people. The French *did* like that all-seeing eye, though. *Vive la révolution!*

In 1812, the United States and Britain were at war *again*. The Americans attacked York, a British city in Canada. The Brits overran Washington, DC, in 1814 and burned the capital in retaliation. Some people thought the British wanted to destroy documents that exposed English Illuminati spies within the US government. Rumor, yes. Evidence? No.

Historical Illuminati conspiracies are just people trying to make sense of nonsense. And in the 1820s, some Americans got carried away. They were so worried about Freemasons taking over that they formed the Anti-Masonic Party.

In 1831, the Anti-Masons held the first presidential nominating convention in the United States. The party didn't last long—but we're still holding those conventions every four years!

**ALL-SEEING EYE?**
CHECK.

**PYRAMID?**
CHECK.

**ROMAN NUMERALS?**
**SOME LATIN STUFF?**
CHECK AND CHECK.

Ergo (that's Latin for *therefore*): The Illuminati *must* have designed America's money.

No go: The Illuminati did not infiltrate the US Mint and force engravers to add their secret codes. Those symbols ended up on our dollar bill in 1935, courtesy of President Franklin Delano Roosevelt! (Full disclosure: FDR *was* a Freemason.) All that stuff came from the Great Seal of the United States. But why was it on the seal?

The Continental Congress wanted a Great Seal that would symbolize the ideals of a new nation. The design actually took six years to figure out.

***ANNUIT COEPTIS* = "PROVIDENCE** (THAT MEANS
"THE PROTECTIVE CARE OF GOD") **HAS FAVORED OUR
UNDERTAKINGS"**

**EYE = PROVIDENCE** (THE EYE OF GOD. SEE ABOVE)
**IS WATCHING OVER THE NEW NATION**

**PYRAMID = STRENGTH**
(THOUGH THOMAS JEFFERSON AND BEN FRANKLIN HAD
WANTED A PHARAOH IN A CHARIOT INSTEAD.)

**THIRTEEN ROWS OF STONE = THIRTEEN AMERICAN COLONIES**
(NOT THIRTEEN ILLUMINATI RANKS. IN FACT, WE DON'T KNOW HOW
MANY RANKS THERE REALLY WERE.)

**MDCCLXXVI = 1776,**
**THE YEAR OF THE DECLARATION OF INDEPENDENCE**
(OKAY, THE ILLUMINATI *WAS* FOUNDED THAT SAME YEAR.)

***NOVUS ORDO SECLORUM* = "A NEW ORDER OF THE AGES"**
(*NOT* "NEW WORLD ORDER")

# FAKE NEWS . . .

## OR IS IT ?

The Bavarian Illuminati's noble, original goal was global revolution in religion and society through moral and spiritual enlightenment.

Okay, shorten "global revolution," etc., to "world domination."

Change "moral" to "money."

And swap "spiritual enlightenment" for "mind control."

*Illuminati confirmed* and still at it . . . or is it?

# SKULL & BONES SOCIETY

This secret society at Yale University was founded in 1832 by a Yale student who traveled to Europe and hung out with someone from a "German society." (*Hmm* ... What German societies come to mind?)

Membership in this Yale club is by invitation only. And, of course, the invitation is wrapped in black ribbon and sealed with a skull and crossbones emblem. New members are called knights; full members are patriarchs; all the rest of us outsiders are vandals.

Bonesmen—no girls! At least not until 1991—meet in "the Tomb," a windowless, stone building with a triple-locked iron door. (The Tomb's address is not so secret: 64 High Street, New Haven, Connecticut—check it out on Google Maps.) Knights get together for dinner, maybe something to drink out of a skull, then perhaps a little lie-down in a coffin while robed patriarchs chant. Sound relaxing? It's not! You have to recite your entire life story while in the coffin!

"THE TOMB" IS THE OLDEST FRATERNITY HOUSE IN THE UNITED STATES THAT'S STILL STANDING.

## 322

Bonesmen say the 322 in their symbol refers to the year the Greek statesman and public speaker Demosthenes died (and that's BCE!). Conspiracy folks say it's about the group's founding in 1832, as the second chapter of a German Illuminati group. Get it? (Hint: Abbreviate the year to '32 and move in another 2 for "second.")

To Bonesmen, 322 is also license to steal license plates with that number.

Skull and Bones originally had a fancy, classical Greek name. But one mischievous member scrawled the spooky skeleton parts on a notice about the club posted at Yale. The rest of the campus was buzzing about it. Though they were supposed to be secretive, club members liked the attention. They renamed themselves the Skull and Bones Society.

Famous Bonesmen include three presidents—William Howard Taft, George H. W. Bush (who was also a head of the CIA), and George W. Bush—as well as supreme court justices, congressmen, governors, secretaries of state, ambassadors, bankers, and lawyers, not to mention the founder of *TIME* magazine, the creator of the Fortune 500 list, and the guy who helped discover Vitamin A. (Just like the Illuminati, Bonesmen are everywhere: government, media, finance, and in most of the other groups named in this chapter.)

It's rumored that there's an infamous skull collection in the Tomb, too. But we'll never know: Members aren't talking. They take an oath to leave the room whenever "Skull and Bones" is mentioned.

# BUTTING SKULLS

## GEORGE BUSH & JOHN KERRY

THE 2004 PRESIDENTIAL ELECTION WAS BONESMAN VERSUS BONESMAN! JOHN KERRY, THE DEMOCRATIC NOMINEE, RAN AGAINST GEORGE W. BUSH, THE REPUBLICAN PRESIDENT.

THE PRESS TRIED TO GET THEM TO TALK ABOUT 322, OR WHETHER SKULL AND BONES HAD SECRET CODES AND HANDSHAKES. BOTH CANDIDATES KEPT QUIET. BUSH SAID, "IT'S SO SECRET WE CAN'T TALK ABOUT IT." (BTW, HE WON.)

# BOHEMIAN GROVE

The Illuminati don't sound like party animals, do they? But a group that's been linked to them sure does.

Bohemian Grove is a private men's club that was founded by journalists and artists in 1872. It supposedly now has 2,500 members. Every July, they get together in a secluded campground deep in a redwood forest near San Francisco, California.

*Hmmm:* The Illuminati started in a forest… right?

The Grovers' bohemian high jinks include drinking, staging musicals, peeing against trees, and burning an *effigy*—a figure that stands in to represent something—in front of a forty-foot stone owl statue.

*Hmmmmm:* The owl is a sign of Minerva, the goddess of wisdom. Minerval is an Illuminati rank, and the owl is one of their symbols… right?

Bohemian Grove's motto is "Weaving

Spiders Come Not Here." That means the happy campers are not supposed to be planning, plotting, or making business deals. But members and their guests include presidents of corporations and countries, generals, Wall Street dudes, and multimillionaires...

*Hmmmmmmmmmmm:* Sounds like Illuminati roll call!

If you want to become a Grover, it's going to cost you around thirty thousand dollars, plus yearly dues. And there's a fifteen-year waiting list to join! Save money: Try getting on the guest list instead.

## DANGEROUS SECRET

IN 1942, THERE *WERE* SOME SPIDERS WEAVING IN BOHEMIAN GROVE. A FEW MEMBERS AND GUESTS BROKE THE NO-BUSINESS RULE. THEY DISCUSSED PLANNING FOR THE MANHATTAN PROJECT, WHICH LED TO THE CREATION OF THE ATOM BOMB.

# THE COUNCIL ON FOREIGN RELATIONS

The website for the Council on Foreign Relations says it exists to help people "better understand the world and the foreign policy choices facing the United States and other countries." Now, skeptics might ask, "What kind of sneaky, secret organization has a website?"

Conspiracy-lovers will answer, "The kind that takes over the world while you're clicking through their website!" They believe the Council on Foreign Relations is part of a global plot. (For more on what that plot is, fast-forward to page 74.)

The council was founded in 1921. World War I had ended three years earlier, and world leaders met in Paris to figure out what might come next. US President Woodrow Wilson proposed an international peacekeeping organization called the League of Nations.

But back home, a group of scholars, military men, and bankers banded together to form the council. They believed the country needed a clear idea of how America should interact with the rest of the world. Ever since, the Council on Foreign Relations has been suspected of pushing its own agendas (its own agendas were based on making lots of money) and/or going for the whole Illuminati enchilada:

WORLD DOMINATION.

You won't be surprised to learn that some of the same movers and shakers who go wild in the redwoods or hail the number 322 also belong to the CFR. You might also find council members on the membership lists of Bohemian Grove or Skull and Bones—*if* you could ever get ahold of those lists!

## COMPLETE THIS SENTENCE:
## THE NEW WORLD ORDER IS

(A) A BRAWLING WRESTLING GROUP HULK HOGAN BELONGED TO.

(B) A HEAVY METAL THRASH BAND.

(C) THE GLOBAL TAKEOVER BY A SECRET GOVERMENT FORMED BY THE ILLUMINATI AND MAYBE ALIENS.

Did you choose (c)? So would nearly one-third of American voters. Okay, maybe they don't all go as far as accepting the aliens, but they do believe the New World Order is about to take over.

So what is the NWO?

It's a bunch of powerful people who plan to run the world for their own benefit. They are, *of course*, part of the Illuminati. They are supposedly using some of the secretive groups you just read about as *fronts*—a sort of camouflage—so the rest of us don't know what's going on. Meanwhile, the NWO is plotting to overthrow all governments, take control of all banking, and build a giant surveillance system to watch everybody in the whole world. That's some to-do list!

# NWO'S *ALLEGED* TRICKS
## TO WATCH OUT FOR

### BAR CODES:

THAT'S HOW THEY'LL KNOW WHAT YOU'RE SPENDING YOUR MONEY ON, SO THEY CAN SELL YOU MORE STUFF.

### SOCIAL SECURITY NUMBERS:

YOU'RE JUST A NUMBER TO THEM . . . WHICH THEY CAN USE TO TRACK YOU.

### MIND CONTROL:

THEY'VE GOT "VOICE TO SKULL" TECHNOLOGY SO THEY CAN BRAINWASH PEOPLE USING MICROWAVE SIGNALS. (UNCONFIRMED WHETHER FLIPPING THIS SWITCH WILL EXPLODE ALL THE POPCORN PACKS IN THE WORLD.)

### JET TRAILS:

WHOEVER ESCAPES THE MICROWAVE BRAINWASH MIGHT BE POISONED BY THE CHEMICALS IN THOSE CONDENSATION TRAILS YOU SEE COMING OUT OF PLANES.

# NWO: NOT SO NEW

On September 11, 1990, President George H. W. Bush addressed Congress and said, "Out of these troubled times, our fifth objective—a new world order—can emerge… An era in which the nations of the world, east and west, north and south, can prosper and live in harmony."

WHOA! Check it out: He said NWO! And on 9/11! *Illuminati confirmed!*

Calm down. George H. W. Bush used "new world order" in a number of his speeches in the 1990s. So did Mikhail Gorbachev, the then-leader of the Soviet Union. And NWO was old news by then, anyhow.

Writer H. G. Wells, who gave us the sci-fi classic *The War of the Worlds*, also wrote a nonfiction book called *The New World Order* in 1939. And twentieth-century leaders like Winston Churchill used the phrase to describe the global changes caused by two world wars.

The New World Order idea isn't exactly new.

# A GLOBAL CONSPIRACY

Think global + act local + tell no one = you're Illuminati. That's what's rumored about the Bilderberg Group. Since 1954, this group of international movers and shakers from government, finance, and industry has met once a year to talk about "major issues facing the world." Or—according to suspicious minds—set up the New World Order.

Some people think everything about the Bilderberg Group is hush-hush. But, actually, you can go on the Bilderberg website and find agendas, meeting locations, and participants' names.

Illuminati hunters also train their all-seeing eyes on other international groups like the United Nations, the Trilateral Commission, and the World Economic Forum in Switzerland. The attendance lists here are also made up of the rich and powerful: all candidates for the puppet masters behind a New World Order.

There *is* a new world order coming… but experts say how we'll live in the future has more to do with technology than with anything else. (Hmmm, could the I in AI also stand for *Illuminati*?)

# RULE THE WORLD?

THERE'S NO PROOF THAT ANY OF THESE GROUPS OF POWERFUL DUDES IS A FRONT FOR THE ILLUMINATI. BUT WHAT WOULD THE WORLD LOOK LIKE IF THE ILLUMINATI REALLY *DID* RUN THE SHOW?

NO MORE CONSPIRACY THEORIES

JAY-Z AND BEYONCÉ WOULD TOUR AS ILLUMINATUS REX AND ILLUMINATUS REGINA

THERE WOULD BE NO COUNTRIES OR NATIONAL BORDERS, ONLY BIG BUSINESS AND SHOPPING ZONES

THE BASIC FOOD GROUPS PYRAMID WOULD BE REVISED TO INCLUDE ONLY DORITOS AND PIZZA BY THE SLICE

SURVEILLANCE CAMERAS AND COMPUTER SCREENS WOULD BE SHAPED LIKE THE ALL-SEEING EYE

EVERYONE WOULD HAVE CLASSICAL NICKNAMES. THERE'D BE A WHOLE LOT OF HERCULES, DEMOSTHENES, CLEOPATRAS, AND ATHENAS RUNNING AROUND.

BLING NAME JEWELRY WOULD GO REALLY BIG

*WEISHAUPT* WOULD REPLACE *HAMILTON* ON BROADWAY

THE OWL WOULD BE THE OFFICIAL BIRD
OF THE WHOLE WORLD

ALL REPTILES WOULD BE FREED FROM
PET STORES, ZOOS, AND TERRARIUMS
(THAT OWL IS GOING TO COME IN HANDY!)

SCHOOL UNIFORMS WOULD INCLUDE
APRONS AND FEZZES.

CLASSES WOULD BE CONDUCTED IN LATIN

WE'D HAVE JET PACKS
(OKAY, NOTHING TO DO WITH THE ILLUMINATI,
BUT THAT WOULD BE COOL, RIGHT?)

CABLE CHANNELS WOULD BROADCAST
*THE SIMPSONS* EPISODE "HOMER THE GREAT" 24/7

EVERYONE WOULD WEAR THE SAME STYLE UNDERWEAR
(BECAUSE THE ILLUMINATI RULES AND CAN MAKE YOU DO
STUPID STUFF!)

POSTAGE STAMPS, COINS, TRAFFIC SIGNS,
PUBLIC SWIMMING POOLS, FLAGS, AND ANY OFFICIAL
LOGOS WOULD BE TRIANGLE-SHAPED

MORE THAN 50 PERCENT OF THE WORLD'S WEALTH
WOULD BELONG TO 1 PERCENT OF THE WORLD'S
PEOPLE. OH, WAIT. THAT ALREADY *IS* TRUE—

# ILLUMINATI CONFIRMED!

## ILLUMINATI CONFIRMED!

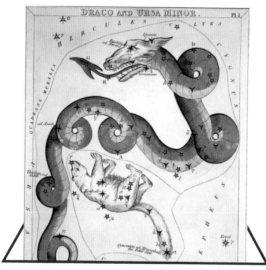

**DRACO IS ONE OF THE LARGEST CONSTELLATIONS. PLENTY OF ROOM UP THERE FOR A REPTOID COLONY.**

Why limit your conspiracy thinking to humans? Maybe the Illuminati were aliens to begin with. Lizard people, anyone?

There is no shortage of internet sites and YouTube videos about shape-shifting alien reptiles. They're hiding as world leaders, corporate executives, and celebrities. They came here from the Draco constellation to enslave us all. They're behind the Illuminati and will be the scaly ones to take over in the New World Order.

Roughly twelve million Americans believe that lizard people are already running the US government! The giveaway clues? Their "love of space and science" and "deep compassion for the fate of mankind." The Illuminati would be okay with those goals.

The slithering masters are also known as reptoids, reptilians, the Reptilian Brotherhood, or Draconians. Or to use the human names of some of them: Queen Elizabeth II, George W. Bush, Barack Obama, Anderson Cooper, Lorde, Mark Zuckerberg, and Hillary Clinton.

So how do these alien creatures shed their skins and become human?

# THEY DON'T.

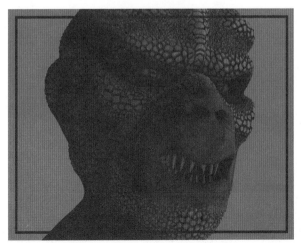

Skin-shedding is so old-school! Reptilians really have crystal skulls. They shoot holograms out of their skulls. (Think mini–Princess Leia popping up in a light beam crying, "Help me, Obi-Wan Kenobi." That's a hologram.) Reptilians cover themselves up in their holograms and—wham! A former snake is now a politician or pop star.

Some conspiracy-watchers believe the Reptilian Brotherhood is a mash-up of Freemasons, the Illuminati, and extraterrestrials.

## L.A. LIZARD PEOPLE

### NO, WE DON'T MEAN MOVIE STARS.

IN 1933, G. WARREN SHUFELT, A MINING ENGINEER, DUG A 250-FOOT SHAFT DEEP UNDER DOWNTOWN LOS ANGELES. HE WAS LOOKING FOR THE LEGENDARY LIZARD PEOPLE—WHAT HE THOUGHT WAS A HIGHLY INTELLIGENT UNDERGROUND CIVILIZATION.

SHUFELT USED A "RADIO X-RAY MACHINE" TO HELP HIM MAP AN AREA OF NINETEEN HUNDRED SQUARE FEET WHERE HE BELIEVED A MAZE OF TUNNELS SNAKED UNDER THE CITY. (NO PUN INTENDED!) THAT'S WHERE SHUFELT THOUGHT THE LIZARD

PEOPLE WERE HANGING OUT WITH THEIR GOLD
AND TREASURES AND VEGETARIAN FOOD SUPPLIES.
ACCORDING TO SHUFELT'S MAP, THE TUNNEL
MAZE WAS SHAPED LIKE A LIZARD, AND HE WAS
DETERMINED TO FIND IT.

HIS EXPLORATIONS WERE A LEAD STORY IN THE
*LOS ANGELES TIMES* NEWSPAPER OF JANUARY 29,
1934. THE ENGINEER DIDN'T FIND ANY TUNNELS OR
TREASURE, AND HIS OWN PROJECT FLOODED. BUT
THE IDEA OF LIZARD PEOPLE DEFINITELY SURFACED!

# THE LONG TALE OF THE

# REPTOID

REPTILIAN-TYPE CREATURES APPEAR IN MANY MYTHOLOGIES FROM ALL AROUND THE WORLD. FOR EXAMPLE: THE EGYPTIAN SERPENT APEP, THE SNAKE IN THE GARDEN OF EDEN, THE AZTEC FEATHERED SERPENT GOD QUETZALCÓATL, THE NAGA GODS OF INDIA, THE DRAGON GODS OF CHINA, THE HOPI SHETI (SNAKE BROTHERS), **OR THE ZULU CHITAULI GODS.**

REPTOIDS ARE ALL THE RAGE NOW, BUT SOME THEORIES SAY THEY'VE BEEN AROUND FOR A LONG TIME. WHICH SENSATIONAL START DO YOU LIKE BEST?

ANCIENT ALIENS CREATED TWO SPECIES TO POPULATE EARTH. HUMANS WERE ON THE LOW END OF THE EVOLUTIONARY SCALE. REPTILIANS WERE ON THE UPPER END—AND THEY ACTUALLY *HAD* SCALES

REPTOIDS EVOLVED FROM DINOSAURS *AND* WERE THE FIRST SPECIES ON EARTH TO MAKE TOOLS

REPTOIDS ARE THE CHILDREN OF HUMANS WHO HAVE MATED WITH WINGED SERPENTS

# KNOW 'EM WHEN YOU

# SSSSEE 'EM

**HERE ARE SOME CLUES SO YOU CAN SPOT THE REPTOIDS AMONG US ... BEFORE THEY SPOT YOU.**

---

**THEY SHAPE-SHIFT.**
(SOME REPTOIDS MAKE POOR CHOICES HERE. SERIOUSLY? YOU'D *CHOOSE* TO TRANSFORM INTO THE BODY OF A NINETY-YEAR-OLD LADY WITH A DORKY POCKETBOOK AND MATCHING HAT?)

**THEY HOP ON DISK-SHAPED CRAFTS INSTEAD OF PUBLIC TRANSPORTATION.**
(CARBON FOOTPRINT, SNAKE DUDE—THINK ABOUT IT.)

**THEY GET IN YOUR HEAD AND MESS AROUND WITH YOUR DREAMS.**
(SO *THAT'S* WHAT THE SCIENCE TEACHER MEANT ABOUT THE "REPTILIAN" PART OF OUR BRAINS ... *RIGHT.*)

**THEY HAVE LOW BLOOD PRESSURE.**
(YO, THOSE REPTILES ARE COLD-BLOODED, TOO!)

**THEY HAVE SMALL, SLITTY EYES.**
(*ANDERSON COOPER?* ... JUST KIDDING!)

**THEY REALLY PRONOUNCE THE S IN WORDS.**
(YESSSSSS! REPTOIDSSSSSSS CONFIRMED!)

# ILLUMINATI

## CONFIRMED

Nowadays, it seems like everywhere you go and everything you do offers new opportunities to wonder: Illuminati confirmed?

There are so many signs to watch for, so many people to keep an eye on, so many secrets to reveal. There's hardly any time to stop and look at the facts!

# I DID IT!

CHECK THE BOXES IF YOU BELIEVE THE ILLUMINATI
IS RESPONSIBLE FOR ANY OF THE FOLLOWING. THE
LIST IS IN ALPHABETICAL ORDER—BECAUSE THERE IS
NO OTHER ORDER THAT MAKES SENSE!

☐ **THE CREEPY CLOWN CRAZE OF 2016**

☐ **DRONES**

☐ **THE EURO AND
THE EUROPEAN UNION**

☐ **FAKING A FAMOUS MUSIC GROUP:
THE BEATLES**

☐ **HIP-HOP**

☐ **HOLLYWOOD**

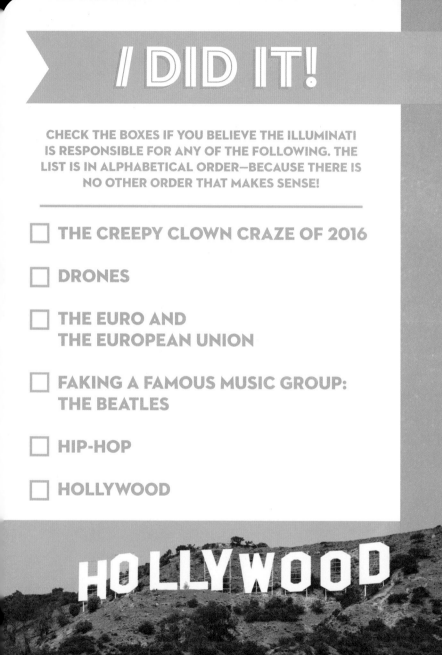

- [ ] **HURRICANES AND EARTHQUAKES**
- [ ] **POISONOUS CLOUD STREAMS FROM JETS**
- [ ] **PUBLIC SCHOOLS**
- [ ] **REALITY TELEVISION SHOWS**
- [ ] **RIGGING THE 2017 SUPER BOWL**
- [ ] **THE SPACE NATION ASGARDIA**
- [ ] **SURVEILLANCE CAMERAS**
- [ ] **TABLOID NEWSPAPERS**

Creepy clowns: Who would have thought?

But the list above is just some of the sneaky ways the Illuminati supposedly distracts us so they can control our minds and take over the world. Is there absolute, verifiable, hard proof of this?

## NOPE. NONE.

But remember how much our brains just love conspiracies? Bring it, I-folks!

# ILLUMINATI?

ABRAHAM LINCOLN ADAM "SPARTACUS" WEISHAUPT ADOLF HITLER AMANDA BYNES ANDREAS SUTOR ANGELA MERKEL ANGELINA JOLIE AUGUSTUS, DUKE OF SAXE-GOTH-ALTENBURG AOL AZEALIA BANKS BARACK OBAMA BARON ADOLF VON KNIGGE BARON DE BASSUS BARON KARL THEODOR VON DALBERG BAUHOF BEYONCÉ BIG K.R.I.T. BILL CLINTON BILL GATES BOB DYLAN BRITNEY SPEARS CHRIS CARTER CHRYSLER DAVID BOWIE DEF JAM RECORDINGS DONALD TRUMP DORITOS EMINEM EMMA WATSON ERNEST II, DUKE OF SAXE-GOTHA-ALTENBURG EXXONMOBIL FORD FRANKLIN D. ROOSEVELT FRANZ ANTON VON MASSENHAUSEN FRIEDRICH NICOLAI GENERAL MOTORS GEORGE GRUNBERGER GEORGE H. W. BUSH GEORGE W. BUSH GEORGE SOROS GISELE BÜNDCHEN GOLDMAN SACHS HALLE BERRY HONDA JAY-Z J. G. HERDER JOHANN ELERT BODE JOHANN COSANDEY JOHANN FRIEDRICH HUGO VON DALBERG JOHANN WOLFGANG VON GOETHE

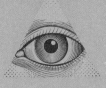

JOSEPH STALIN JOSEPH VON UTZSCHNEIDER JUSTIN BIEBER KANYE WEST KARL AUGUST, GRAND DUKE OF SAXE-WEIMAR-EISENACH KATY PERRY KESHA KIM KARDASHIAN LADY GAGA LEBRON JAMES LIL WAYNE MADONNA MAX ELDER VON MERZ MAYER AMSCHEL ROTHSCHILD MCDONALD'S MICHAEL JACKSON MIKHAIL GORBACHEV MILEY CYRUS MOUNTAIN DEW NICKI MINAJ POPE FRANCIS PRINCE CHARLES OF HESSE-KASSEL PRINCE LICHNOWSKY QUEEN ELIZABETH II RIHANNA RONALD REAGAN SEAN COMBS TARGET THERESA MAY TOM BRADY TUPAC SHAKUR USAIN BOLT WILL.I.AM WINSTON CHURCHILL XAVER ZWACK

NOTICE ANYTHING ABOUT THE NAMES IN WHITE?
WHAT DO A COUPLE OF JOHANNS AND VONS SOUND LIKE
TO YOU? KIND OF GERMAN, BAVARIAN-ISH, RIGHT? THESE
ARE THE ONLY NAMES ON THIS LIST THAT ARE ILLUMINATI
CONFIRMED! THEY WERE MEMBERS OF THE ORIGINAL
BAVARIAN ILLUMINATI.

Let's not forget that the Illuminati were Freemasons. And Freemasons were originally just that: stonecutting builders. So it's no surprise that conspiracy-seekers can find geographical evidence of the Illuminati. And their favorite location is Washington, DC.

YOU SEE IT CLEARLY, RIGHT? THE GROUNDS OF THE US CAPITOL BUILDING WERE DESIGNED IN THE SHAPE OF AN OWL! YUP, THE BIRD THAT'S THE SIGN OF MINERVA AND ALL OVER THE PAMPHLETS OF THE BAVARIAN ILLUMINATI.

THIS MASSIVE MASONIC HOUSE OF THE TEMPLE IS
THIRTEEN STREETS AWAY FROM THE WHITE HOUSE.
THE BUILDING HAS THIRTY-THREE COLUMNS AND A
BEAUTIFUL STAINED GLASS WINDOW WITH AN
ALL-SEEING EYE.

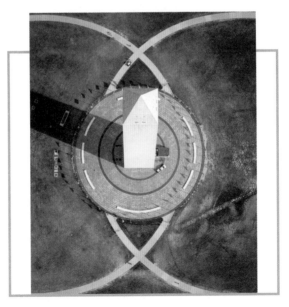

SEEN FROM ABOVE, THE WASHINGTON MONUMENT
FORMS A "POINT IN A CIRCLE" SYMBOL. THIS IS JUST
LIKE THE ⊙ SYMBOL THAT THE ILLUMINATI USED AS
CODE FOR THEMSELVES.

THE SOUND OF I-MUSIC | THE SOUND OF I-MUSIC | THE SOUND OF I-MUSIC | THE SOUND OF I-MUSIC | THE SOUND OF I-MUSIC | THE SOUND OF I-MUSIC | THE SOUND OF I-MUSIC | THE SOUND OF I-MUSIC | THE SOUND OF I-MUSIC | THE SOUND OF I-MUSIC | THE SOUND OF I-MUSIC | THE SOUND OF I-MUSIC | THE SOUND OF I-MUSIC | THE SOUND OF I-MUSIC | THE SOUND OF I-MUSIC | THE SOUND OF I-MUSIC | THE SOUND OF I-MUSIC | THE SOUND OF I-MUSIC | THE SOUND OF I-MUSIC | THE SOUND OF I-MUSIC | THE SOUND OF I-MUSIC | THE SOUND OF I-MUSIC | THE SOUND OF I-MUSIC | THE SOUND OF I-MUSIC | THE SOUND OF I-MUSIC | THE SOUND OF I-MUSIC | THE SOUND OF I-MUSIC | THE SOUND OF I-MUSIC | THE SOUND OF I-MUSIC | THE SOUND OF I-MUSIC | THE SOUND OF I-MUSIC | THE SOUND OF I-MUSIC | THE SOUND OF I-MUSIC | THE SOUND OF I-MUSIC | THE SOUND OF I-MUSIC |

# THE SOUND OF
# I-MUSIC

THE SOUND OF I-MUSIC | THE SOUND OF I-MUSIC | THE SOUND OF I-MUSIC | THE SOUND OF I-MUSIC | THE SOUND OF I-MUSIC | THE SOUND OF I-MUSIC | THE SOUND OF I-MUSIC | THE SOUND OF I-MUSIC | THE SOUND OF I-MUSIC | THE SOUND OF I-MUSIC | THE SOUND OF I-MUSIC | THE SOUND OF I-MUSIC | THE SOUND OF I-MUSIC | THE SOUND OF I-MUSIC | THE SOUND OF I-MUSIC | THE SOUND OF I-MUSIC | THE SOUND OF I-MUSIC | THE SOUND OF I-MUSIC | THE SOUND OF I-MUSIC | THE SOUND OF I-MUSIC | THE SOUND OF I-MUSIC | THE SOUND OF I-MUSIC | THE SOUND OF I-MUSIC | THE SOUND OF I-MUSIC | THE SOUND OF I-MUSIC | THE SOUND OF I-MUSIC | THE SOUND OF I-MUSIC | THE SOUND OF I-MUSIC | THE SOUND OF I-MUSIC | THE SOUND OF I-MUSIC | THE SOUND OF I-MUSIC | THE SOUND OF I-MUSIC | THE SOUND OF I-MUSIC | THE SOUND OF I-MUSIC | THE SOUND OF I-MUSIC | THE SOUND OF I-MUSIC | THE SOUND OF I-MUSIC | THE SOUND OF I-MUSIC | THE SOUND OF I-MUSIC | THE SOUND OF I-MUSIC | THE SOUND OF I-MUSIC | THE SOUND OF I-MUSIC | THE SOUND OF I-MUSIC | THE SOUND OF I-MUSIC | THE SOUND

*"Illuminati want my mind, soul, and my body*
*Secret Society trying to keep an eye on me."*

—Mobb Deep's Prodigy, "I Shot Ya (Remix)," 1995


*"Y'all haters corny with that Illuminati mess."*

—Beyoncé, "Formation," 2016


Enough said.

# RAP REVELATIONS

The late rapper Prodigy, of Mobb Deep, was the first to mention the notorious Big *I* in song. The Illuminati conspiracy then spread through the hip-hop world and on to mainstream pop music.

In the 1990s, rap stars from Dr. Dre to CeeLo Green to the Wu-Tang Clan warned about the Illuminati and the New World Order they were plotting. There were whispers that Tupac Shakur had sold his soul to the Illuminati for his mighty talent. And then there were rumblings that the Illuminati were behind the drive-by shooting that killed him.

## BEHIND THE LYRICS

Some scholars have studied how *oppression*—a very real experience, especially for people of color—is explained and expressed in different ways, including conspiracy theories. Questions about racism, inequality, authority, power, and control are important subjects in the world of hip-hop and rap music. Some artists and their audiences find the answers in conspiracies, and so references to the Illuminati and the New World Order show up in their lyrics.

Even though they are all talented, hardworking artists on their own, the Illuminati is what's *supposedly* behind the success of Michael Jackson, JAY-Z, Beyoncé, Kanye West, Nicki Minaj, Rihanna, Miley Cyrus, Lady Gaga, Britney Spears, Madonna, and Katy Perry. Why? So the shadowy secret society can control their fans and followers! The internet offers a lot of so-called "proof":

## SUPER BOWL HALFTIME SHOWS

THE STAKES ARE HIGH. OVER ONE HUNDRED MILLION PEOPLE WATCH. IF YOU'RE THE STAR OF THE SHOW, YOU CAN KEEP 'EM TALKING THE NEXT DAY IF YOU WORK IN A FEW ILLUMINATI SIGNS.

### 2013:
DOUBLE WHAMMY—BEYONCÉ FLASHES THE TRIANGLE SIGN *AND* THE STADIUM LIGHTS LATER GO OUT IN THE THIRD QUARTER. I-POWER!

### 2015:
KATY PERRY WEARS A DEVIL-FLAME BODYSUIT AND RIDES IN ON A TIGER MADE OF *TRIANGLES*.

### 2017:
LADY GAGA. ENOUGH SAID.
PLUS, THERE WERE PENTAGRAMS EVERYWHERE.

# ROC THE TRIANGLE

## WHEN WE SAY, "ILLUMINATI," YOU SAY, "JAY AND BEY."

JAY-Z and Beyoncé are under constant surveillance. Everybody's watching.

All because of a simple hand sign that went viral.

In 1995, JAY-Z formed a record label called Roc-A-Fella with two other partners. Roc-A-Fella put out JAY-Z's rap albums. The label produced other up-and-coming stars such as Kanye West. (Also branded as Illuminati.) JAY-Z and his partners wanted to build a successful business, which they did.

"Roc-A-Fella" was a cool take on being "Rockefeller rich"—meaning having the bucks of John D. Rockefeller. (Also branded as Illuminati.) He was an oil business hotshot of the nineteenth and early twentieth century who became one of the richest men in the world.

Early in the twenty-first century, JAY-Z started flashing his now famous triangle at concerts. He's explained many times that it's a diamond. He was hoping the Roc-A-Fella albums would "go diamond," which means sales of ten million records. Audiences dug the hand signal, so JAY-Z kept doing it. And then other performers mimicked the move.

Rap is notorious for its rivalries. Some artists accused JAY-Z and Beyoncé of ties to the Illuminati. Other artists saw that Illuminati stuff could be played for all it's worth in lyrics and videos.

But *hello*? Can we just please accept that JAY-Z is saluting his businesses—which now include the media empire Roc Nation—not sending brainwashing Illuminati signals?

# TOP OF THE

# ILLUMINATI CHARTS

| ARTIST | PYRAMID | TRIANGLE | TRIANGLE HAND SIGN | TRIPLE SIX HAND SIGN |
|---|---|---|---|---|
| BEYONCÉ | X | X | X | X |
| MILEY CYRUS | X | | | X |
| DRAKE | | | X | X |
| EMINEM | | X | | X |
| JAY-Z | | | X | X |
| LADY GAGA | X | X | | X |
| KATY PERRY | X | X | | X |
| RIHANNA | X | X | X | X |

MANY ARTISTS WHO TOP THE MUSIC CHARTS MAKE HEADLINES WHEN THEY PERFORM OR RELEASE MUSIC VIDEOS WITH SIGNIFICANT SYMBOLS. *ILLUMINATI CONFIRMED!* HERE'S A CHART OF WHO'S USED SYMBOLS OF THE SECRET SOCIETY IN THEIR VIDEOS OR CONCERTS.

| ALL-SEEING EYE | COVERED EYE | OWL | REPTILES | OTHER WEIRD STUFF |
|---|---|---|---|---|
| X | X | X | X | SOMETIMES CALLED THE "QUEEN OF THE ILLUMINATI" |
| X | X | | | HER EYELIDS SUPPOSEDLY PROVE SHE'S A REPTOID |
| | X | X | | WEARS A $120,000 DIAMOND OWL NECKLACE |
| X | X | | | MAY NOT BE WHO—OR WHAT—HE SEEMS. SEE PAGE 104 |
| | X | | | CREATED THE TRIANGLE HAND SIGN |
| X | X | | | EVERYTHING IN HER CLOSET |
| X | X | | X | SAID SHE'D BE WILLING TO JOIN THE ILLUMINATI—IF IT EXISTED |
| | X | | | SOMETIMES CALLED THE "PRINCESS OF THE ILLUMINATI" |

# OUR WORLD OF SECRET STUFF

OUR WORLD OF SECRET STUFF | OUR WORLD OF SECRET STUFF | OUR WORLD OF SECRET STUFF | OUR WORLD OF SECRET STUFF | OUR WORLD OF SECRET STUFF | OUR WORLD OF SECRET STUFF | OUR WORLD OF SECRET STUFF | OUR WORLD OF SECRET STUFF | OUR WORLD OF SECRET STUFF | OUR WORLD OF SECRET STUFF | OUR WORLD OF SECRET STUFF | OUR WORLD OF SECRET STUFF | OUR WORLD OF SECRET STUFF | OUR WORLD OF SECRET STUFF | OUR WORLD OF SECRET STUFF | OUR WORLD OF SECRET STUFF | OUR WORLD OF SECRET STUFF | OUR WORLD OF SECRET STUFF | OUR WORLD OF SECRET STUFF | OUR WORLD OF SECRET STUFF | OUR WORLD OF SECRET STUFF | OUR WORLD OF SECRET STUFF | OUR WORLD OF SECRET STUFF | OUR WORLD OF SECRET STUFF | OUR

You can find references to the Illuminati, the Freemasons, and the New World Order *everywhere*. We're talking not just hip-hop and pop music, but all of pop culture: movies, books, ads, TV shows, fashion, video games, and, of course, the internet.

~~Illuminati~~ *Nothing* confirmed, though.

# ABCs OF THE

**BIG I**

YOU'D NEED AN ENTIRE ENCYCLOPEDIA TO FIT IN ALL THE
ILLUMINATI-INSPIRED, SECRET SOCIETY STUFF THAT SURROUNDS
US. WOULD YOU SETTLE FOR AN ABECEDARIUM INSTEAD?
(SOUNDS VERY ENLIGHTENED, YES?
IT MEANS AN ALPHABET BOOK.)

## A
### *ASSASSIN'S CREED*
One of the best-selling video games of all time. The killer As are in
a shadowy war with the Knights Templars; the Illuminati is implied.
Bracers on, watch that hidden blade!

## B
### DAN BROWN
His books *Angels & Demons* and *The Da Vinci Code* are filled with
secret society misinformation.

## C
### CBS LOGO
Come on now, you can see it's a giant eye!

## D
### *DUCKTALES*
Check that eye chart in the background of this
Disney cartoon closely.

## E
### EMINEM
He just might be an Illuminati clone. (Pretty wack even for
conspiracies!)

## F
### FINGER
Where Miley Cyrus has a tattoo of an eye. Evil? All-seeing? DKDC.

## G
### GUARDIAN ANGELS
The badge of this now international safety patrol that started in
New York City has an all-seeing eye in a triangle.

## H
### HORSE SCULPTURE AT DENVER INTERNATIONAL AIRPORT
A thirty-two-foot-tall blue mustang with glowing red eyes that locals call "Blucifer." The New World Order supposedly has bunkers underneath the airport.

## I
### ILLUMINATI
Whoever, wherever they are, they own this letter!

## J
### BET YOU WERE EXPECTING JAY-Z HERE, BUT WE NEEDED HIM FOR Z. GIVE IT UP FOR JUSTIN BIEBER INSTEAD.
More than three million people viewed a YouTube video of him blinking. That's supposed to prove he is a reptoid. Yup, blinking: the thing we all do about fifteen to twenty times a minute!

## K
### KENZO WORLD PERFUME
Its ad directed by Spike Jonze ends with a soaring dancer bursting through a giant eye.

## L
### LARA CROFT, TOMB RAIDER
The game. The movie.
Just starring in it made Angelina Jolie a suspected Illuminati.

## M
### MARVEL COMICS: NEW AVENGERS SERIES
The Illuminati are superheroes, what else?

## N
### *NATIONAL TREASURE*
You got your Knights Templar, your Freemasons, and a hero named Benjamin Franklin Gates. Not subtle, but still funny.

## O
### OOSTERBEEK, THE NETHERLANDS
Where the secret Bilderberg Group meets at the very public Hotel de Bilderberg.

## P
### PROGRESSIVE INSURANCE
Its TV ad pokes fun at the Illuminati . . . *or does it?*

## Q
### QUEEN OF THE ILLUMINATI
Is it Beyoncé? Rihanna?
Queen Elizabeth II (who actually *is* a queen)?

### R
## RUSSIAN HACKING
Doesn't this have KGB *and* NWO written all over it?

### S
## *SPONGEBOB SQUAREPANTS*
Sure, he's a square, but watch for those triangles in the background!

### T
## TRIANGLE
Duh!

### U
## UMBERTO ECO'S NOVEL *FOUCAULT'S PENDULUM*
Read it when you're older.

### V
## VATICAN SECRET ARCHIVES
Historical documents from the last twelve centuries that take up fifty *miles* of shelves. Supposedly, it's all under the control of the Illuminati.

### W
## ROBERT ANTON WILSON
He wrote *The Illuminatus!* with Robert Shea. This 1975 cult classic has it all: the Illuminati, JFK assassination, Masons, Mafia, terrorist attacks, and a character who travels in a submarine made of gold. It helped launch the age of popular conspiracy novels.

### X
## *THE X-FILES*
Conspiracy, yes. Illuminati, no.
But everybody knows the theme song.

### Y
## YOUTUBE VIDEOS
There are nearly twenty-six million of them on the New World Order, six million of them about the Illuminati, and over a million about the Freemasons.

### Z
## JAY-Z
The man behind the triangle.

# HUM THAT TUNE!

COMPOSER MARK SNOW WROTE THE THEME SONG FOR THE POPULAR TV SERIES *THE X-FILES*. ITS SIGNATURE SPOOKY SOUND WAS CREATED WITH A SYNTHESIZER THAT USED AN EFFECT CALLED "WHISTLING JOE."

*THE X-FILES* IS ABOUT TWO FBI AGENTS WHO INVESTIGATE UNSOLVED PARANORMAL CASES, CONSPIRACIES, AND ALIENS. THE AGENTS UNCOVER A SHADOWY GOVERNMENT PLOT TO KEEP THE EXISTENCE OF EXTRATERRESTRIAL LIFE A SECRET.

THE ILLUMINATI IS NOT MENTIONED IN *ANY* OF THE SERIES' 208 EPISODES. BUT ALIEN REPTOIDS, ON THE OTHER HAND . . .

# KEEP YOUR EYES
# OPEN

Adam Weishaupt's Bavarian Illuminati had a secret sign, that dot in a circle. It symbolized knowledge, spreading outward. Because the original Illuminati were all about reason and knowledge.

But today's conspiracy thinking goes round and round in circles: If you can't prove a conspiracy, it's because the Illuminati are hiding the truth. And if you disprove a conspiracy, it's because the Illuminati *wants* you to think that.

You have to keep your eyes—and your mind—open!

## ENLIGHTEN YOURSELF

# HOW TO TELL IF SOMEONE IS ILLUMINATI

☑ THEY DENY IT

☑ THEY HAVE A TRIANGLE, PYRAMID, EYE, OR STAR IN THEIR LOGO

☑ THEY HAVE A TRIANGLE, PYRAMID, EYE, OR STAR TATTOO

☑ THEY HAVE TRIANGLE, PYRAMID, EYE, OR STAR JEWELRY

☑ THEY ARE FAMOUS AND HAVE BEEN PHOTOGRAPHED WITH A HAND COVERING ONE EYE

☑ THEY ARE FAMOUS AND FORM A FINGER TRIANGLE ON ANY OCCASION, ESPECIALLY IF THERE'S A CAMERA OR SMARTPHONE AROUND

☑ THEY DON'T DENY IT

YOU CAN EASILY FIND COUNTLESS WEBSITES, BOOKS, VIDEOS, OR PHOTOGRAPHS THAT SUPPORT THIS CHECKLIST. THERE ARE QUIZZES ON WHETHER YOU SHOULD JOIN THE ILLUMINATI OR WHAT LEVEL ILLUMINATI YOU'D BE IF YOU SIGNED UP. THERE ARE "OFFICIAL" ILLUMINATI WEBSITES, FACEBOOK PAGES, AND TWITTER ACCOUNTS.

YOU CAN'T MAKE THIS STUFF UP . . . *OR CAN YOU?*

IF YOU WANT TO KNOW IF THE TRUTH IS OUT THERE, YOU NEED TO KNOW HOW TO LOOK.

# READ WITH A SKEPTICAL, ALL-SEEING EYE

Don't just look for facts that fit your ideas.
Look for the ones that *don't*. Compare.

# BEWARE OF FAKE NEWS

Legit info is usually found in more than one media source. "More than one" does *not* mean more than one pal retweeted the same hashtag item or shared the same Snapchat story. Keep clicking.

# SAYS WHO?

Look for copyrights and the name of the person who wrote a post, article, or book. Find out who owns, publishes, or posts the info you're reading. Who's selling ads on it?

# USE COMMON SENSE

If something seems wack—like, why would a secretive society recruit me through an online form?—trust your instincts. Keep **reading** (and don't give them any personal information).

## IN CONCLUSION:

IF SOMEONE TELLS YOU HE'S A
REPTILIAN ILLUMINATI OVERLORD,
ASK TO SEE HIS FORKED TONGUE!